DISCARD

D0824513

MONEY MATH

Math and My World

Kieran Walsh

Rourke
Publishing LLC
Vero Beach, Florida 32964

www.rourkepublishing.com

PHOTO CREDITS:
Cover photo by The Image Works.com. All other photos from AbleStock.com, except for pages 35, 41, 45 by the author; illustration of hands with money © Getty Images

Editor: Frank Sloan

Cover and Interior design by Nicola Stratford
Page layout by Heather Scarborough

Library of Congress Cataloging-in-Publication Data

Kieran Walsh

Walsh, Kieran.
  Money math / by Kieran Walsh.
      p. cm. -- (Math and my world)
Includes bibliographical references and index.
Contents: Allowance -- Part-time jobs -- Full-time jobs -- Taxes --
Banks -- Currency -- The stock market -- Gross domestic product.
  ISBN 1-58952-381-4 (hardcover)
  1. Mathematics--Study and teaching (Elementary)--Juvenile literature.
2. Money--Juvenile literature. [1. Mathematics. 2. Money.] I. Title.
II. Series: Walsh, Kieran. Math and my world.
  QA135.6.W33 2003
  513--dc22
                              2003011560

Printed in the USA

w/w

TABLE OF CONTENTS

INTRODUCTION

Money is something that you probably have a lot of experience with even if you've never given it much thought.

For instance, have you ever received money for your birthday or Christmas? Maybe you wanted to spend it right away, but your parents told you to "save it for a rainy day."

That was good advice. The fact is, "money doesn't grow on trees." This is another expression you may have heard your parents use. It's a way of saying that money is hard to come by.

If you have ever owned a piggy bank, then you already have some experience with managing money. ▶

Adults say these things because they know how important money is. Money is what we use to buy the clothes we wear, the food we eat, and the homes we live in. In many respects, the amount of money we have, and our ability to manage it sensibly, determines our quality of life.

Managing money effectively requires using a lot of math. Paying bills can be a lot easier with the aid of a calculator.

ALLOWANCE

Unlike your parents, you don't go to work yet because you're busy with school. But this doesn't mean you never work. You probably do work all the time. Maybe you even get paid for it.

For the time being, your only "job" is going to school. But that doesn't mean you don't work. Can you think of work you do on a regular basis that doesn't involve school?

Doing chores around the house is work.

Maybe every time you mow the lawn, or vacuum, or shovel snow, or wash the dishes, your parents give you a little money.

Another possibility is that you do these chores, but instead of paying you every time you do a chore, your parents give you a little payment every week. This is called an **allowance**.

If your parents give you $5 a week for washing dishes, how much money will you have earned at the end of three months?

Let's say that your parents give you an allowance of $2 a week. If you didn't spend any of it, how much money would you have at the end of a year? You can find out by using multiplication.

There are 52 weeks in one year, so:

$$2 \times 52 = 104$$

At the end of a year, you would have earned $104 from your allowance. It's not as much as your parents earn, but it's pretty good for washing dishes!

On the other hand, it might not be practical to save all of the money you earn. You might want to spend some on things you enjoy, like movies, or candy, or comic books.

Let's say that instead of saving all your money, you use a little bit every time you get paid to buy things you really want.

What if, for every $2 of allowance you received, you were to save only half of it and use the rest for spending money? How much would you have saved by the end of the year?

You can figure this out by using division. First of all, you know that if you saved all your allowance money you would end up with $104 in a year. To find out how much you will have saved if you only keep $1 a week, all you have to do is divide 104 in half.

$$104 \div 2 = 52$$

So, if you use half of your allowance for spending money and put the other half aside, you would have $52 at the end of a year's time. That's money you could use for a bigger purchase like a skateboard, or a video game, or—and it's important to remember this option—you could just keep saving it.

As you grow up and you are able to take on more responsibilities, you will likely have to do more chores. Likewise, your allowance will probably grow to take into account all the new work you are doing.

The point is, the numbers, like your responsibility, will grow, but the principles you've seen here will remain the same for the rest of your life. Just as earning is the first stage of money, figuring out how much of your earnings you can comfortably spend is the second stage.

The typical price for a compact disc is about $16. If your allowance is $8 a week, how many CDs could you buy at the end of a four-week month?

Income

Anything that provides you with money is a *source of income*. This includes your allowance and any other work you do that earns money. Sometimes the chores you do at home can expand into the outside world. For example, a busy neighbor who doesn't have time to do his own mowing might ask you if you could mow his lawn. Or, if you've grown up taking care of a baby brother or sister, other families in your community might ask you to baby-sit for them occasionally. How much would you charge for the following jobs?

Shoveling snow

Walking dogs

Raking leaves

If you were earning money from these tasks on a regular basis, how much would you be earning along with your allowance?

PART-TIME JOBS

Typically, any job that involves a working schedule of 40 hours a week or more is considered a full-time job. Meanwhile, a job that involves, say, 25 hours of work every week is a part-time job.

Also, full-time jobs are usually only performed during the workweek, which is Monday through Friday. There are seven days in a full week, but a workweek only involves five days. Part-time jobs are a lot more flexible. Because there are fewer hours, they may be divided up in different ways, including working late at night or on weekends. Of course, not all full-time jobs have regular hours. Doctors and nurses, for instance, work odd hours, as do janitors.

People take part-time jobs for a variety of reasons. Many college students work part-time jobs to help pay for their education. Teenagers still in high school might work part-time jobs because, as they've gotten older, their tastes have become more expensive. If you want to buy a car, or a stereo, or a pricey item of clothing, you're going to need more than $2 a week.

Bear in mind, though, that even as the amounts of money grow, the ideas remain the same. Although you never thought of it that way before, the $2 a week you earned for doing chores is a **salary**—a payment for work done on a regular basis.

Likewise, you will be paid a salary for working a part-time job. The salary for a part-time job is usually expressed in terms of *dollars an hour.*

If you were to apply for a part-time job, you would encounter a concept called minimum wage. Simply put, this is the lowest amount of money that an employer can pay you for your work. Minimum wage varies from state to state, but as of 2003, the minimum wage for most states is typically around $5.15. If you were working at a job that only paid the minimum wage, you would be earning five dollars and fifteen cents an hour.

◀ *As you get older your tastes will change. Getting into sports like skateboarding, for instance, is expensive. How long would it take you to buy a skateboard with your income?*

What if your job pays $5.15 an hour and you have a 20-hour workweek? How much money do you earn in a week?

You can calculate the answer by multiplying:

$$5.15 \times 20 = 103.00$$

A job that pays $5.15 an hour with a 20-hour workweek pays $103.00 a week. Taking it a step further, how much does this job pay in a year?

Just multiply the amount of money you would earn in one week ($103) by the number of weeks in one year (52):

$$103 \times 52 = 5356$$

So, in a year's time, a job that pays $5.15 an hour and involves a 20-hour workweek would earn you a total of $5,356.

Five thousand dollars might seem like a lot of money to you now, and it certainly is a lot more than the $104 dollars a year you were earning from an allowance. In a moment, though, you'll be dealing with even larger numbers. As you deal with bigger and bigger salaries, remember that your expenses — the money you have to pay to live—go up as well.

Time is money. If you have a part-time job that pays $7 an hour, and you work every day from 1:00 p.m. to 5:00 p.m., how much money do you earn in a day? ▶

FULL-TIME JOBS

If a typical full-time job is 40 hours a week, and a full-time job is only done 5 days a week, how many hours a day is a person required to work?

This is a problem you can solve with division. Divide the number of hours in a workweek (40) by the number of days a week you would be required to work (5):

$$40 \div 5 = 8$$

Full-time jobs pay more than part-time jobs, but they also require harder work and more responsibility.

So, a working day is eight hours. If you've ever heard anyone use the phrase, "9 to 5," now you know what they mean.

As an adult, your salary is no longer expressed as dollars an hour. It is expressed as a figure, like $20,000, $40,000, $60,000.

What do these numbers mean? They are actually a way of expressing the amount of money a person earns in a year's time.

To demonstrate, let's do some math to figure out how many hours a year the average person works.

There are 52 weeks in a year. You also know that a full-time job is about 40 hours a week:

$$52 \times 40 = 2080$$

In other words, in a single year, the average person works about 2,080 hours. Just to keep things really simple, let's drop the 80 from that figure. That will give you a nice, round number of 2,000 hours a year.

The next step will involve division. If a person earns a salary of $40,000 a year, how much money are they earning every hour?

$$40,000 \div 2000 = 20$$

So, a salary of $40,000 a year is really the same thing as earning $20 an hour. You can see, though, that with numbers this large, it is a lot easier to just express the result as $40,000 a year.

After all, at this stage of life, you're going to be spending most of your time at work, so it's more efficient to think in terms of large chunks of time.

We have been discussing salary as dollars per year, but this doesn't mean you have to work for an entire year before you get paid. Most employers pay their workers at regular intervals, or periods of time. Pay periods vary from company to company. People who are paid once a week are paid weekly. People who are paid every other week are paid bi-weekly.

At a salary of $40,000, how much can a person expect to be paid if his or her employer issues payment on a weekly schedule? Remember, there are 52 weeks in a year, and again, just for the convenience of using a round number, let's make it 50:

$$40,000 \div 50 = 800$$

So, for people making a salary of $40,000 a year and who are paid on a weekly schedule, their typical paycheck will be about $800.

What about employees at the same salary on a bi-weekly schedule? All you have to do is deal with half the number of weeks:

$$40,000 \div 25 = 1600$$

So their typical paycheck would be $1,600.

Different Salaries

Not everyone earns the same amount of money. Here are a few examples of average salaries per year for different professions:

Accountant – $150,000

Architect – $105,000

Chef – $60,000

Firefighter – $50,000

Movie Star – $35,000,000

Office Manager – $35,000

By subtracting, can you calculate how much more per year an accountant earns compared to a chef? What about an architect compared to an office manager?

Not everyone earns the same salary. People in manual labor, or blue-collar jobs, like this factory worker, earn less than people in office, or white-collar, jobs.

TAXES

Unlike the money you made from your chores, you don't actually get to keep everything you've earned from the salary of a part-time or full-time job.

At first, this might sound unfair. But it all makes sense when you learn where the money is going. In order to pay for the services we are provided, like mail, public construction, the fire department, and the police, a portion of your salary is taken by the government. This is called taxation.

The fire department is one of many public services, including the police and the mail, that are paid for with taxes. Can you think of others? ▶

Much like minimum wage, the actual amount of taxes a working adult has to pay depends on many factors. As a rule of thumb, though, most people calculate their taxes by estimating that a quarter — or 25% — of their income will go to the government.

Just as an example, let's use the $40,000 a year salary again. How much of that would be paid in taxes?

Actually, there are a couple of different ways to do this.

You could multiply $40,000 by .25, the decimal expression of 25%:

$$40,000 \times .25 = 10,000$$

By doing that, you have determined that for a salary of $40,000 a year, about $10,000 will have to be paid in taxes.

Another way of solving the same problem would be to divide $40,000 by 1/4.

$$40,000 \div 1/4 = 10,000$$

Either way, you get the same result—the portion of a $40,000 salary that will go to taxes is $10,000.

How much money does that leave you with?

$$40,000 - 10,000 = 30,000$$

$30,000.

Next, let's consider how taxes affect our weekly, or bi-weekly paychecks. We'll continue using the $40,000 base for calculations. Earlier, you learned that a $40,000 salary paid at weekly intervals would be about $800 a week. What about after taxes?

$$800 \times .25 = 200$$

and then

$$800 - 200 = 600$$

After taxes, your paycheck would be roughly $600.

For a bi-weekly payment scheme:

$$1600 \times .25 = 400$$

and then

$$1600 - 400 = 1200$$

With a salary of $40,000 paid on a bi-weekly basis, you would earn about $1,200 every other week.

Take-Home Pay

Working people refer to the money that is left after their taxes have been paid as *take-home pay*.

Let's say that your allowance is $3 a week. If you had to pay taxes on that money, what would your take-home pay be? You can find out by determining what one-quarter of 3 dollars is, and then subtracting that amount from 3 dollars:

$$3 \times .25 = .75$$
$$3 - .75 = 2.25$$

So your take home pay would be $2.25 a week! How would that change affect your saving and buying habits?

BANKS

Banks might seem mysterious, but they are really just safe places where people can keep the money they have earned.

Do you have a place where you keep all your money? You probably do, whether it's in a plastic bag, or a shoebox under your bed, or a coffee can in your bedroom closet.

Banks, though, can do many things that a bag, or shoebox, or coffee can can't do. If you go to a bank, you'll notice that there are guards on duty. Also, the money in the bank is stored in large vaults. These are ways of protecting your money from being stolen.

Along with the greater security a bank offers, banks can charge and pay **interest**. Interest is, in one sense, a way of using money to make money. You see, although they might not look like stores, banks are places where people can buy money.

But why would someone want to buy money?

All the time, people have to make big purchases like cars, or businesses, or homes. If you had to buy a home, how would you do it? One possibility would be to save money gradually until you had enough.

Homes are very expensive, though. It would take many years for the average person to save enough money to buy one. The other option would be to go to a bank and apply for a **loan**. With a loan, your parents could buy their home right away and then pay back the money they owe to the bank over time.

The way banks make money on a loan is by charging interest. The Federal Reserve, the "head" bank of the United States, sets the amount of interest a bank can charge on a loan.

Without the help of a loan from a bank, it would take a very long time for a family to earn enough money to buy a home.

This is called the interest rate, and the amount is expressed as a percentage—4%, 5%, 6%, and so on. The interest rate is constantly changing, but you will hear the term annual interest rate. This is because the interest for a loan is calculated over the period of one year.

What if you were to take out a loan of $10,000 at an annual interest rate of 4%? How much would you owe the bank at the end of a year? You can figure it out in three steps:

1) Convert the interest rate (4%) to a decimal number by dividing 4 by 100:

$$4 \div 100 = .04$$

2) Then multiply the amount of the loan by this number

$$10,000 \times .04 = 400$$

3) Then add this result to the amount of the loan

$$10,000 + 400 = 10,400$$

So, for a loan of $10,000 at an annual interest rate of 4%, you would owe $10,400 at the end of a year.

The good thing about banks is that while they charge interest, they also pay interest. There are different types of accounts that you can set up at a bank. A checking account is basically like a large wallet. But a savings account will pay interest on the money you have stored there. The interest rates for accounts are always lower than for loans, but it's more than you can get from a shoebox!

CURRENCY

Have you ever seen money from another country? It looks very different than the money we use in the United States. Sometimes the bills are larger, or more colorful, and they have different pictures and words printed on them.

In America the money we use is the U.S. dollar. The dollar is printed in different amounts ranging from 1 to 100. The dollar bills being printed today include 1, 5, 10, 20, 50, and 100. Apart from bills, there are also coins. There are four different types of coins, each with a different value:

Quarter = 25 cents

Dime = 10 cents

Nickel = 5 cents

Penny = 1 cent

People do math every day with these different bills and coins. For instance, what if you wanted to buy a T-shirt that costs $20? How could you pay for that T-shirt using $5 dollar bills?:

$$20 \div 5 = 4$$

You would need 4 $5 bills to buy a $20 T-shirt.

If you have ever traveled outside the United States, you know that to purchase goods in another country you have to use that country's **currency**, or type of money. There are almost as many different currencies as there are countries. Just to name a few examples, Great Britain has the pound, Mexico has the peso, and Japan has the yen. Likewise, other countries have their own coinage.

Not all monies are equal. For instance, one U.S. dollar is not the same as one Japanese yen. The worth of a country's money has to do with many things, including the prosperity of the country, its political stability, and other factors.

American currency is divided into bills and coins. If a dollar bill is worth 100 cents, then how many quarters equal one dollar? How about nickels?

When countries that use different currencies do business, they rely on the exchange rate, or rate of exchange. This is how countries that use different currencies pay each other.

Again, because the worth of a country's money is always changing, so too is the exchange rate. Just for your own calculations, though, let's say that the exchange rate for the British pound is $1.60.

In that case, about how much does an item worth 10 pounds cost in dollars?

In order to find out how many dollars 10 pounds is, you need to use multiplication. By referring to the exchange rate, you know that a pound is worth about $1.60:

$$10 \times 1.60 = 16.00$$

An item costing 10 pounds is worth about $16.

Bear in mind, though, that this is only an example. If you were to look up the current exchange rate for the British pound, it might be more or less than $1.60. The point is, the worth of money is constantly changing.

What about the things that people buy, though? Do their prices change? Yes, they do. In fact, some things people buy have different prices every day of the year!

Welcome to the world of **stocks**!

The Euro

"Euro" is short for "Europe." The Euro became the official currency of Europe in January 2002. The twelve European countries that agreed to use the Euro were Austria, Belgium, Finland, France, Germany, Greece, Ireland, Italy, Luxembourg, the Netherlands, Portugal, and Spain. In the past, if you lived in one of those countries and traveled to another, you would have to use a different currency. The Euro replaced all of these countries' currencies, including the Greek drachma, which had been in existence for about 2,650 years.

The Euro pictured here is a 50-cent piece. If a Euro is equal to 100 cents, how many of these would you need to make one Euro?

THE STOCK MARKET

Have you ever seen a stock **market** before? It's a market where people can buy (and sell) stocks. Sometimes, the stock market is referred to as the stock exchange. There are three big stock markets in the United States. The biggest is the NYSE, the New York Stock Exchange. Next is the AMEX, the American Stock Exchange. Finally, there is the NASDAQ, or the National Association of Securities Dealers.

The New York Stock Exchange is also called the NYSE. The NYSE is one of three big stock exchanges in the United States. ▶

What exactly are stocks? Stocks are portions of a company. If a person owns stock in a company, he or she actually owns a small part of that company. Stockowners are often called **shareholders**.

Stock prices are not fixed. Instead, stocks are bought and sold using an **auction** method. When a certain stock is very popular and everyone wants to buy it, the price of that stock goes up. On the other hand, if a stock isn't popular the price goes down.

To find out how much a stock costs, you will need to refer to a stock listing. You can find stock listings in the business section of any large newspaper. Take a look at one and see if you can understand what it all means. It probably seems very confusing. But hang on, everything will get clearer.

Stock reports look confusing at first, but with a little math they begin to make sense. ▶

Pay particular attention to the numbers on the left. The first column is labeled as "52-Week High," and the second is "Low."

That phrase, "52-Week" should remind you of something. Yes—52 weeks is the number of weeks in one year. So, a stock's "52-Week High" is the highest price a stock has sold at in the past year. Meanwhile, the "Low" is the lowest price it has sold for in the past year.

Again, it's important to point out that you don't want to generalize too much with stocks. Stocks change all the time, but using these two numbers, you can get a pretty decent picture of a stock's price.

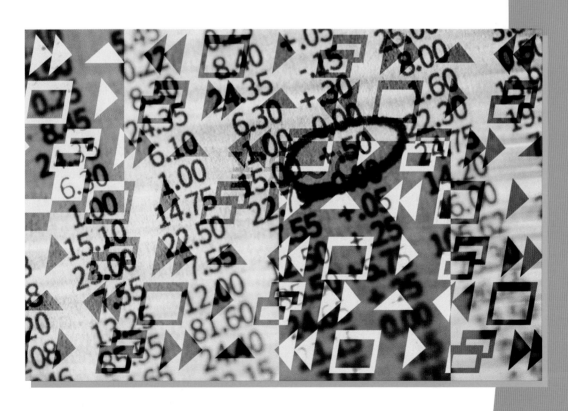

For instance, let's say that a stock's "52-Week High" is 70 (dollars) and its "Low" is 30 (dollars). Using those two numbers, what is the average price of the stock? To find out, you need to do two operations:

Add the two numbers together:

$$70 + 30 = 100$$

Divide the result by 2 (the number of addends):

$$100 \div 2 = 50$$

Therefore, the stock's average price is about $50.

Why would anyone want to own stocks? Remember, by owning shares of stock, you own a small part of a company. As part owner of a company, if the company turns a profit, you are entitled to a portion of that profit. These profits are called **dividends**.

Let's refer to the stock listing again. Toward the middle you will see a number labeled "Yield." This number, expressed as a percentage, is the amount of profit a stock produces, or yields, per share.

What if you owned 1,000 shares of stock in a company that had a 2% yield? How much money would your stocks have produced?

First, convert the percentage to a decimal number:

$$2 \div 100 = .02$$

Then multiply your number of shares by the result:

$$1000 \text{ x } .02 = 20$$

So your stock has made $20 of profit for you!

These are the basics of stock prices and stock earnings, but in real life, stocks are not this simple. Unfortunately, you can lose money in the stock market, and the only way to make a big profit is to take a big risk.

Because stocks are so risky, people who buy them watch their performance carefully. Have you ever heard of the Dow Jones Industrial Average, or the Standard and Poors 500, or the Russell 2000 Index? These are actually averages of the performance of a number of different stocks. The Dow Jones is an average of the prices of 30 different stocks. Likewise, the Standard and Poors number is an average of 500 different stocks, while the Russell 2000 Index is an average of 2,000 stocks.

Depression and Recession

What happens in the stock market affects the entire world. A *crash* is when people sell their stocks in great numbers and, as a result, the stocks and the companies they represent are worthless. The result of the stock market "crash" in 1929 was a period of worldwide crisis known as the Great Depression. Another, far less destructive, stock market crash took place in 1987. A depression is a prolonged recession, or downturn in economic growth. A recession generally lasts about six to eighteen months, while a depression can go on for many years.

GROSS DOMESTIC PRODUCT

Has your family ever held a garage sale? Probably, before the sale started, you put a price tag on every item so that the people who came to look would see what everything cost.

What if you were to add up the price tags for all the items at your yard sale? What would everything be worth altogether?

The idea behind **Gross Domestic Product** (GDP) is a little bit like that. Clearly, in order to sell goods to other countries, a country has to produce goods. A country's gross domestic product is the total value of all the goods and services a country produces. For the most part, GDP is measured on a yearly basis.

The items at your yard sale would probably add up to a few hundred dollars. The numbers for GDP are much larger. The estimated GDP for the United States in 2001 was *$10,082,000,000,000—that's ten trillion eighty-two billion dollars!* *Source—World Almanac 2003

The idea behind Gross Domestic Product (GDP) is a little bit like adding up the worth of all the goods at your family's yard sale. Instead of just a yard sale, though, the GDP measures the worth of all the goods in the country!

Usually, just to make things easier, the GDP number is expressed in billions of dollars. For instance, the above number would be:

10,082

To get the full number again, all you would have to do is multiply this number by 1 billion:

10,082 x 1,000,000,000 = 10,082,000,000,000

The United States is the leading country in the world as far as GDP is concerned. In 2001, China was in second place with a GDP of 5,560 billion dollars.

How many more billions is the 2001 U.S. GDP worth?

$$10,082 - 5,560 = 4,522$$

So, in 2001, the United States had a GDP worth 4,522 billion dollars more than China.

Like everything else to do with money, a country's GDP is always changing. If things are going well, the GDP grows. For example, the GDP for the United States in 2000 was $9,824.6. The next question is, by how much did the GDP for the United States grow in 2001?

$$10,082 - 9824.6 = 257.4$$

In 2001, the GDP for the United States grew by $257,400,000,000!

Gross National Product

The Gross Domestic Product became the official measure of the United States economy in 1991. Up until that time, the measure was the Gross National Product (GNP). The difference between the two involves where money is earned. The Gross National Product was the measure of the total profits of a country's citizens, whether they were living in that country or not. The GNP is still used, but the GDP is the statistic you'll hear most often.

◄ *Can you think of some of the products produced by China that gave it the second-highest Gross Domestic Product for 2001?*

CONCLUSION

By this point, you're probably thinking about ways that you can manage the money you earn differently. Maybe, for instance, you'll start saving more. Or perhaps you'll consider using your money to buy things that could help you to earn more money. If you have a paper route, for instance, you might want to get a new bike.

Maybe you'll even explore the possibility of opening your own checking account. Or perhaps you'll open a savings account to put money aside for a stereo, or a car, or your education…

Now that you've read this book, what's the first thing you plan to do with your money?

Managing your money doesn't mean that you have to think about it all the time, but you'll start to find that there are reminders everywhere! ▶

GLOSSARY

allowance – an amount of money given to you from your parents on a regular basis, often as payment for doing household chores

auction – a method of selling where the goods go to the highest bidder

currency – the particular type of money a country uses

dividends – the money owed to a shareholder if a stock earns a profit

gross domestic product – the total economic output of a country; the total worth of all the goods produced by a country in a year

interest – money charged on a loan, or the money earned on funds in a savings account

loan – money borrowed from a bank in order to make a large purchase, like a car or a home

market – a place where goods are bought and sold

salary – a payment for work done on a regular basis

shareholders – people who own shares, or small portions, of a company

stocks – shares of a company

Further Reading

Cooper, Jason. *American Bills and Coins.* Rourke Publishing, LLC, 2003.

Cooper, Jason. *Around the World With Money.* Rourke Publishing, LLC, 2003.

Cooper, Jason. *How Coins and Bills are Made.* Rourke Publishing, LLC, 2003.

Cooper, Jason. *Keeping Money Safe.* Rourke Publishing, LLC, 2003.

Cooper, Jason. *Money Through the Ages.* Rourke Publishing, LLC, 2003.

Cooper, Jason. *Paying Without Money.* Rourke Publishing, LLC, 2003.

Zeman, Anne and Kate Kelly. *Everything You Need To Know About Math Homework*. Scholastic, 1994.

Websites to Visit

http://www.howstuffworks.com/bank.htm
How Stuff Works – How Banks Work

http://www.howstuffworks.com/stock.htm
How Stuff Works – How Stocks and the Stock Market Work

http://www.kidsmoney.org/
Kids' Money

http://www.summerjobs.com/
Summer Jobs

INDEX

About the Author

Kieran Walsh has written a variety of children's nonfiction books, primarily on historical and social studies topics, including the recent Rourke series *Holiday Celebrations* and *Countries in the News*. He divides his time between upstate New York and New York City.